"Welcome Aboard!"
Introducing the Crew Aboard the Good Ship 'Scooter'

and "The First ART LESSON"

Written & Illustrated by Fayrene Parrish©

ISBN 978-0-9826717-2-6

TABLE OF CONTENTS

The Shipmates Motto
Honor the specialness of each person.
Celebrate individual uniqueness.
Live in harmony with all.

Some Boating History

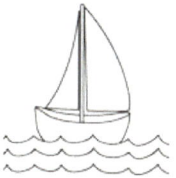

According to archeology*, Boating goes back to at least 6,300 B.C. That's a very, very long time ago. Archeologists discovered a 'dugout' boat, carved from a tree. Apparently 'sails' were not yet used at that time in history.

Jump ahead a couple thousand years, and it was discovered that long, very narrow boats were made in Egypt and crossed the waters by 'oarsmen' rowing those boats.

Then 'sail-making' came along, and they were added to help the boats go faster, using the wind instead of only oarsmen.

As time continued, the countries around the Mediterranean all contributed improvement to the building and rigging of boats. They became Merchant/Cargo Ships....AND were up to 70+ feet long and about 16-18 feet wide!...and still oarsmen still rowed on each side.

Sailing had become the major form of transportation by about 1200 A.D. Countries far apart began to interact, and exchange, and more and more places were discovered.

It's what brought Columbus to North and South America.

So, Sailing - Boating, is a major part of our World's history.

*Archeology, is a Noun; the study of human history and prehistory through the excavation of sites and the analysis of artifacts and other physical remains.

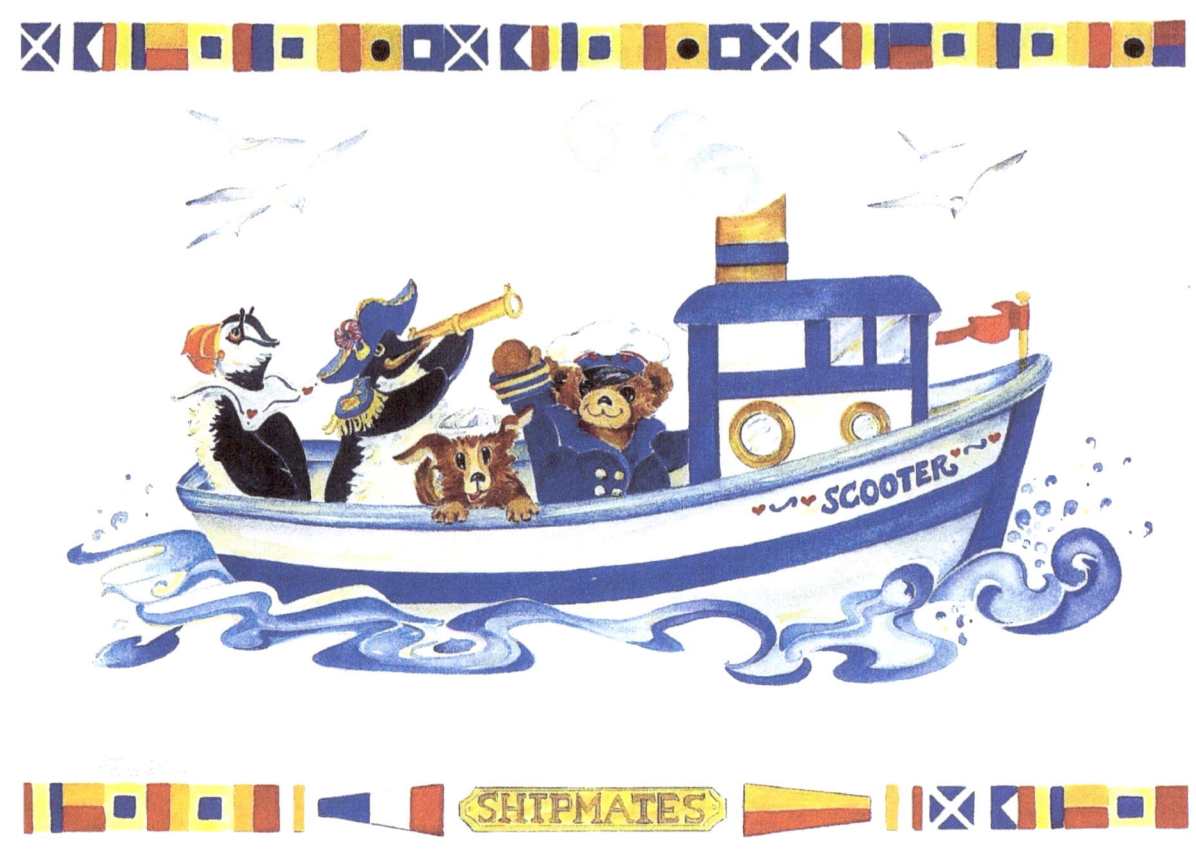

Welcome Aboard!

We're called 'The Shipmates', the jolly crew aboard the good ship 'Scooter'. Please join us as we explore the world with our 'Learning Adventures.

We'll meet wonderful animals and people, go special places, and have exciting, fun filled adventures as we meet critters and plants that grow and live in beautiful places called "Habitats".

But first, we would like to introduce ourselves and meet you.

So, let's start on the next page where you can color our pictures with your crayons.

Use your imagination. Have fun. This is
your show!

First...
Lay your crayons out beside you. You will be using these colors for this first
"Learning Adventure'

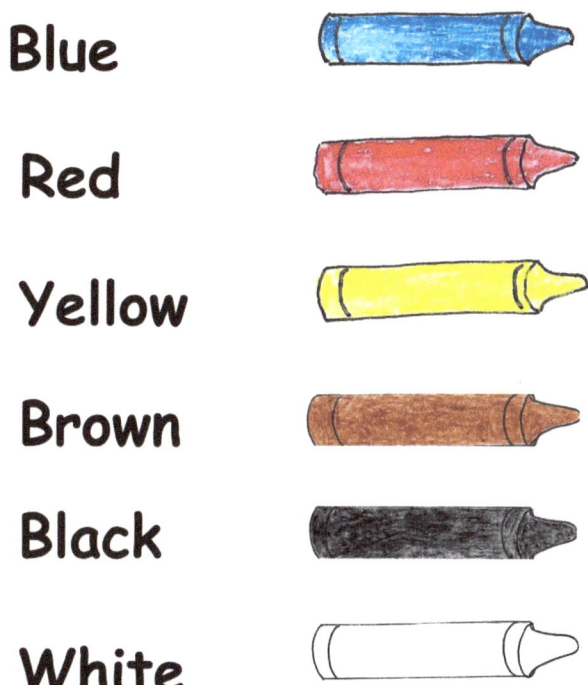

Blue

Red

Yellow

Brown

Black

White

Note: You can see us, in full color, as individual Shipmates, on page 7.

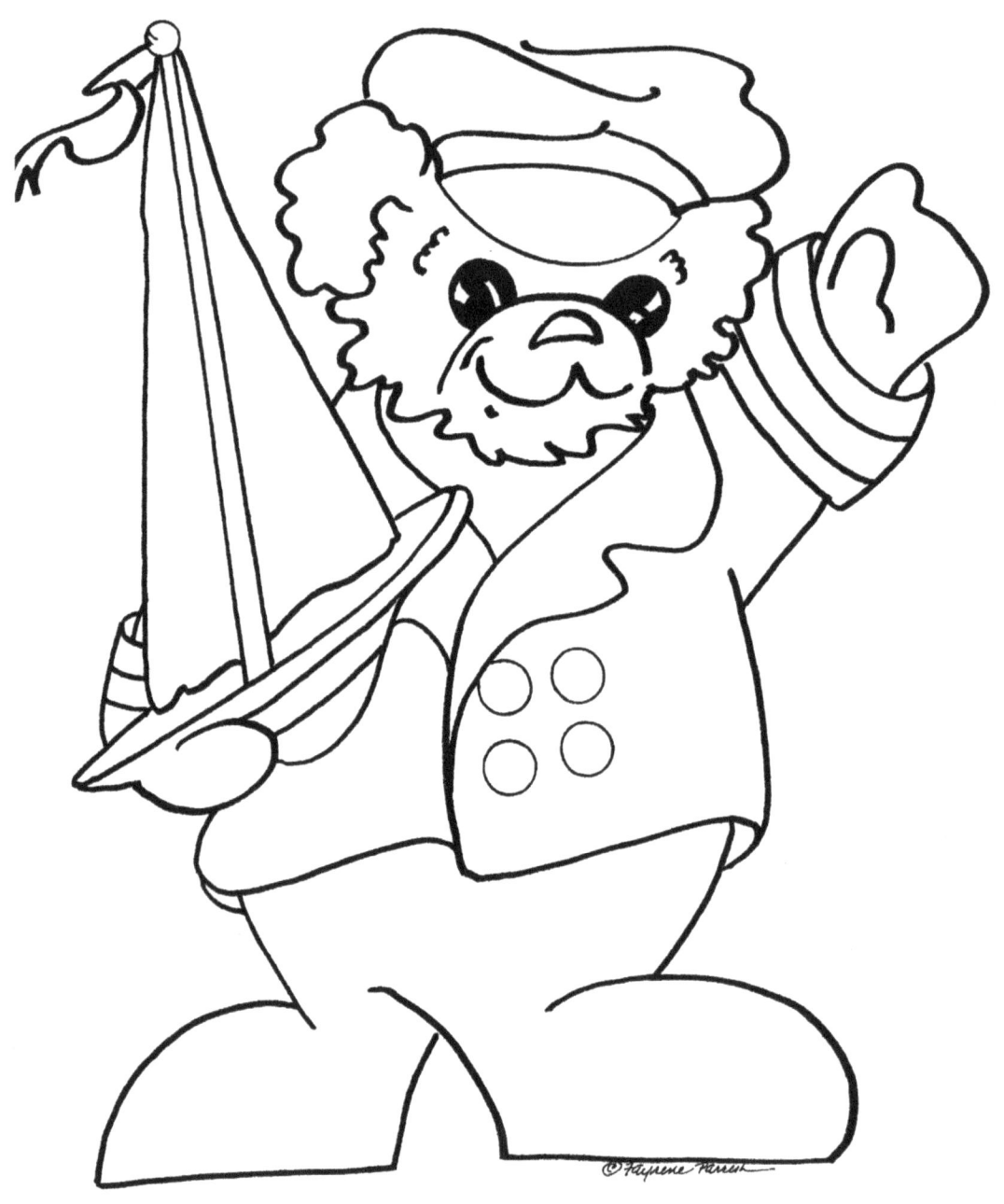

Captain Bear

"Hi!" I'm Captain Bear the skipper of the good ship 'Scooter'. With my jolly crew of sea-going mates, we roam the Oceans of the World in search of adventure and magical lands.

3

'Pancho', The Salty Sea Dog,

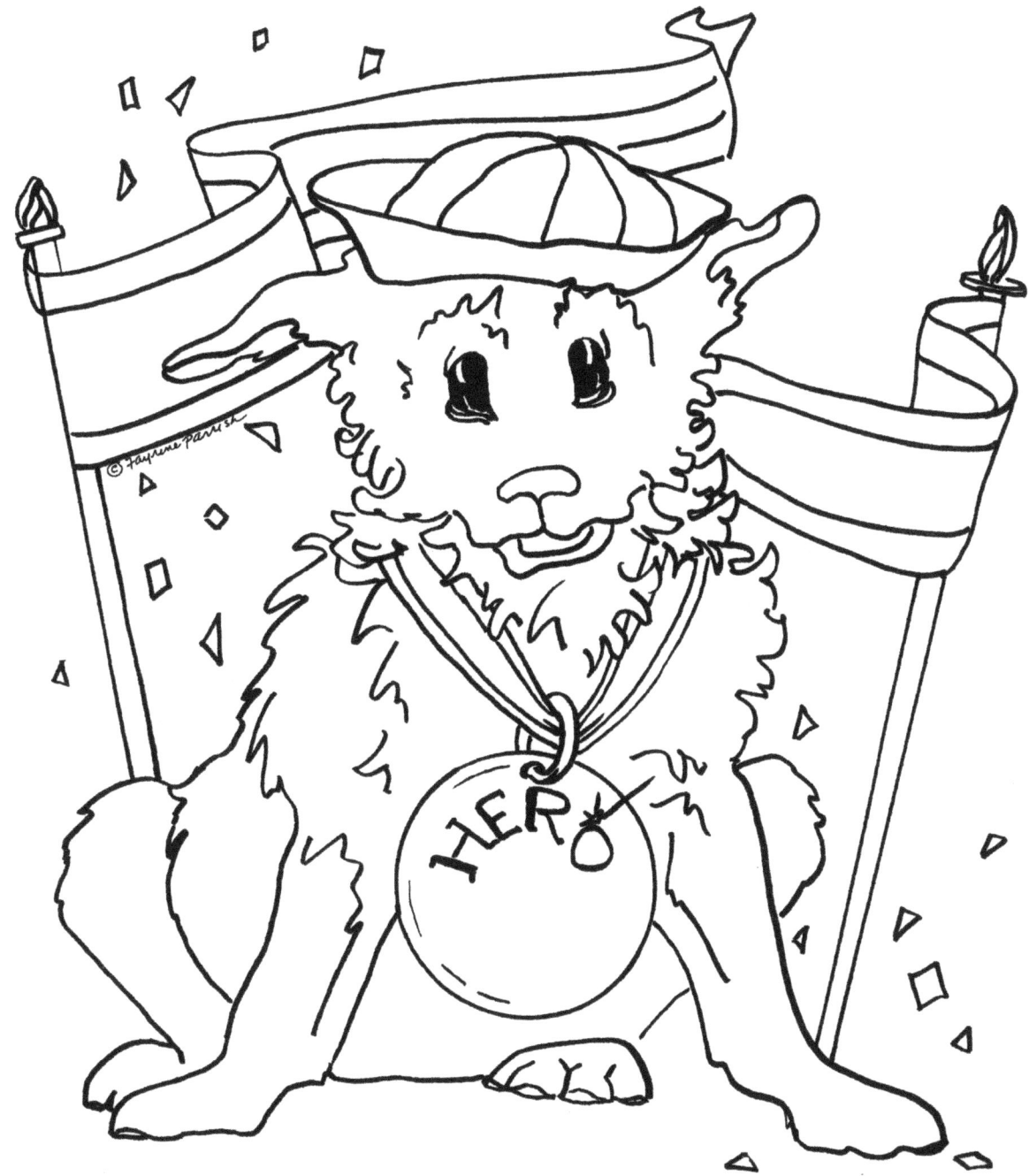

...is the First Mate aboard 'Scooter, and hero of many adventures. He loves hiking and exploring and is the hero of many a tale.

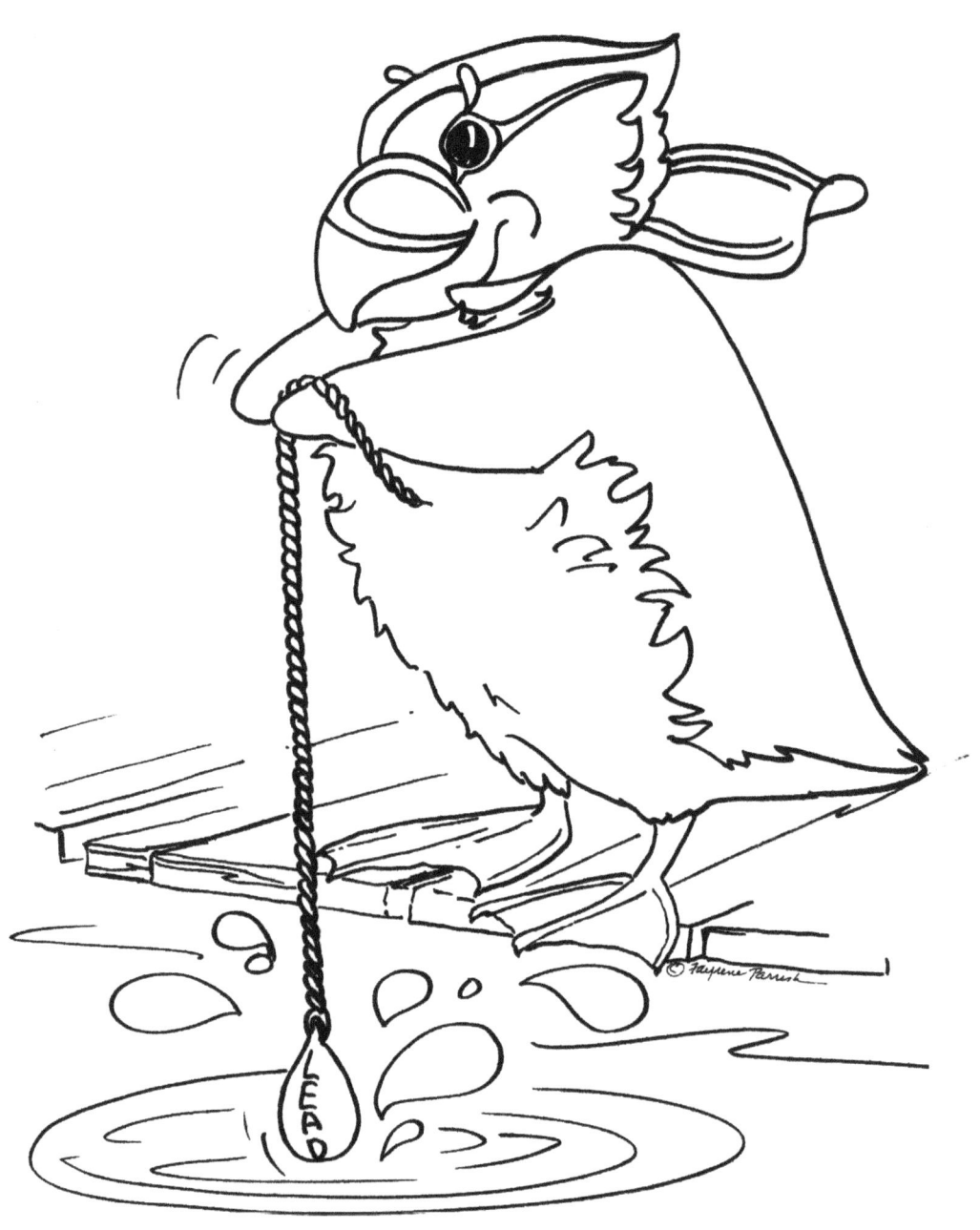

Huff'N Puffin, the Navigator aboard 'Scooter'.

Huff'n Puffin is navigator aboard the good ship "Scooter". He draws a chart of each and every Voyage.

He is also an art teacher, and will be teaching an introduction to the 'Magic of Art' in the next chapter.

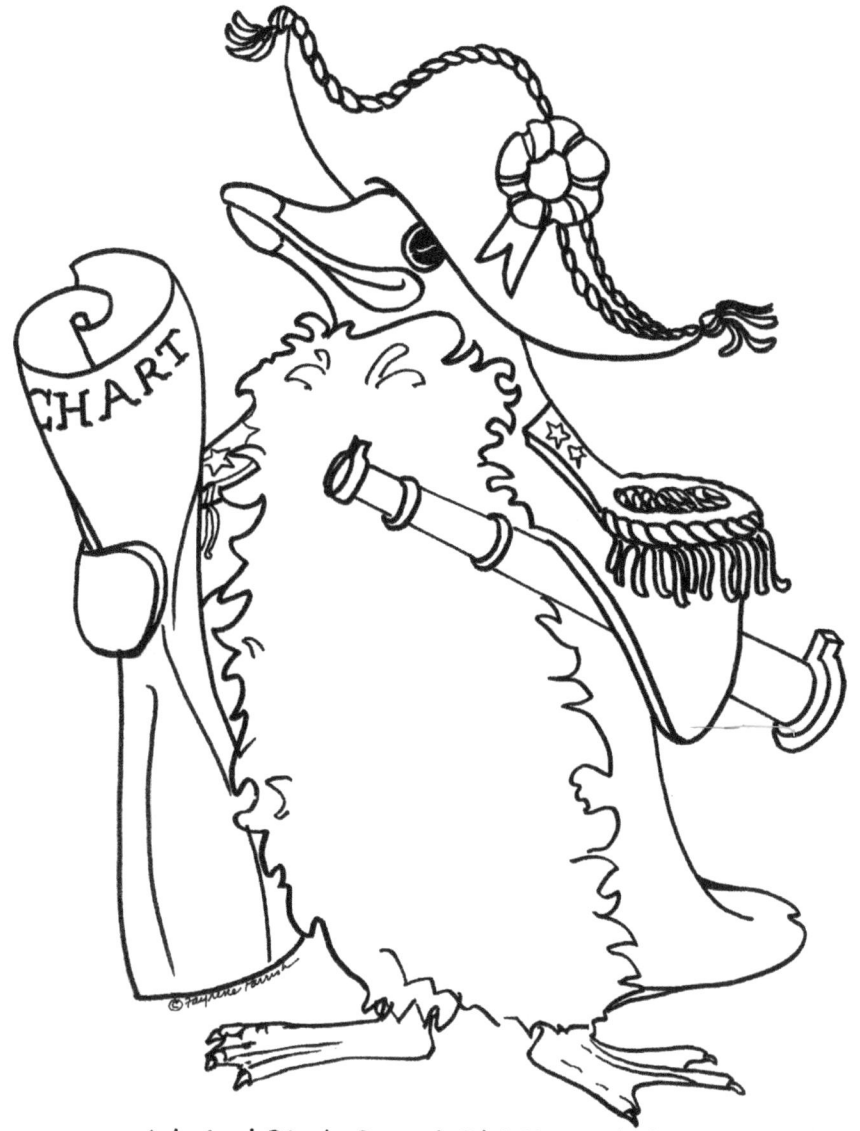

Admiral Bird, Grand Old Man of the Sea

I'm Admiral Bird. I've traveled to many a foreign land while sailing the seas. With my bright telescope, I'm always looking for new places to explore. My hobby is sharing "Nautical History", and I have plenty of tales to share.

Thanks for coloring and getting to know us. We've been around many a year - first as original art, then posters, note cards, special stories commissioned to support unique events and places....we've even been invited to share our adventures in school room classes. Now, we're 'Coloring Books' - telling 'stories' that we call 'Learning Adventures'. Hope these pictures will help you as you through this introduction.

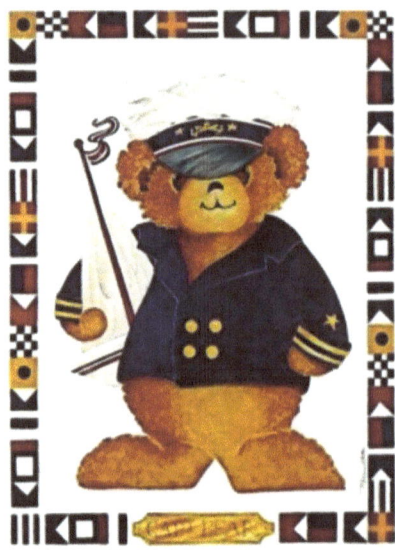

Captain Bear

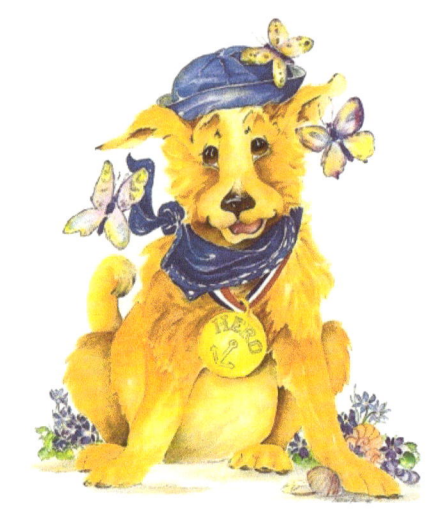

Pancho the Salty Sea Dog

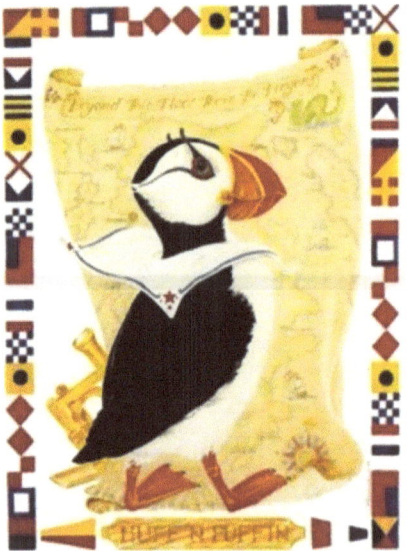

Huff'n Puffin

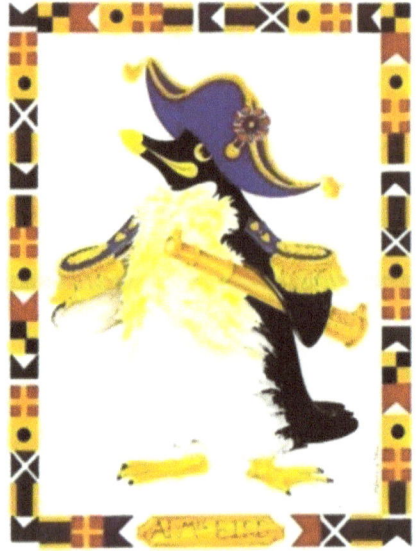

Admiral Bird

Chapter 2
"The Magic of Color" - our First Art Lesson

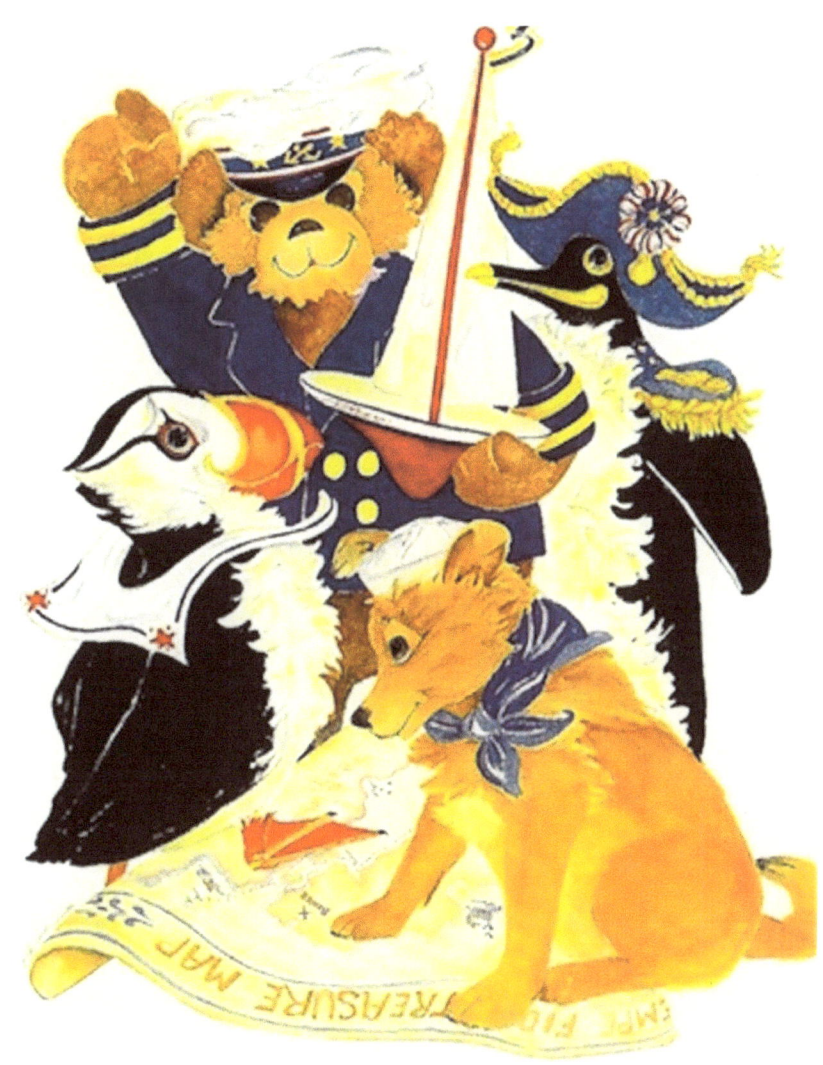

Huff'n Puffin, our navigator aboard the good ship 'Scooter', loves Art. He draws all our Navigational Charts and loves to share his knowledge about the
'Magic of Color'.

So, let's explore the excitement you will find in the many colors all around us!

...Let's get started.

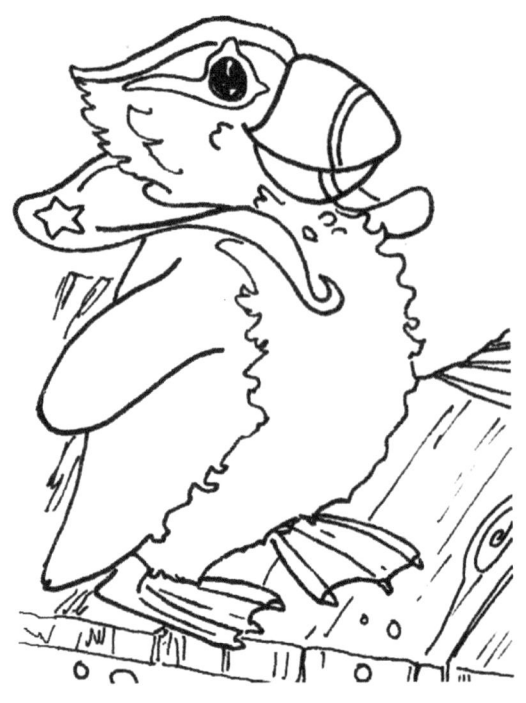

Ahoy, Mates! My name is Huff'n Puffin. I'm the Navigator aboard the good ship 'Scooter'. It's my job to draw all the charts for our journeys. So, because I like to draw, and especially to Color....I'm going to show you some great 'tricks' for coloring with crayons.
It's Magic!

First, pick any color crayon.

Now color this Balloon....

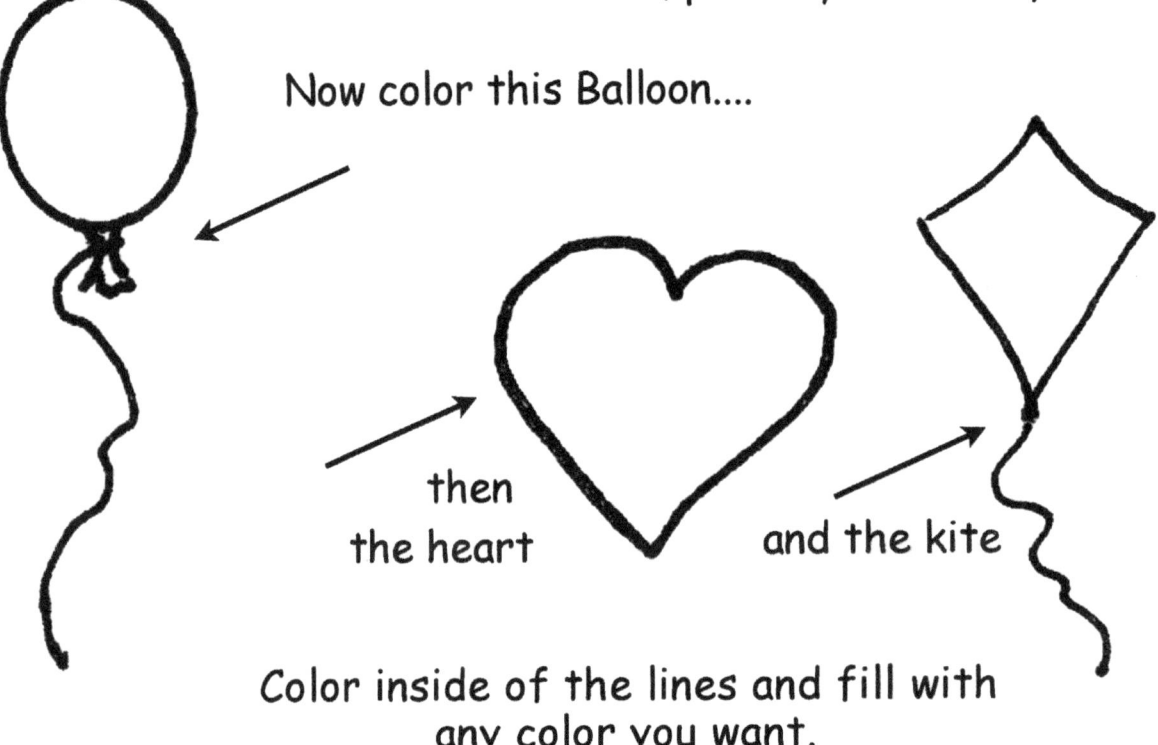

then
the heart

and the kite

Color inside of the lines and fill with any color you want.

This is Your Show!

You're doing good!   So, let's learn what colors can do.

First, color this circle
with the **BLUE** crayon.

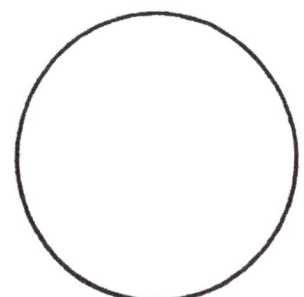

Next, color this circle
with the **YELLOW** crayon.

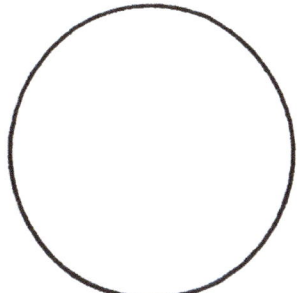

Then, color this circle
            with the **Red** crayon

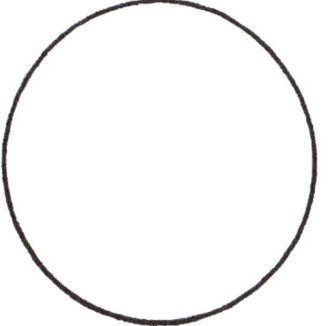

Okay Mates, now the 'Magic' begins. You have
Blue Yellow and **Red** colors in the first three
circles.

10

They are called the 'Primary' Colors.

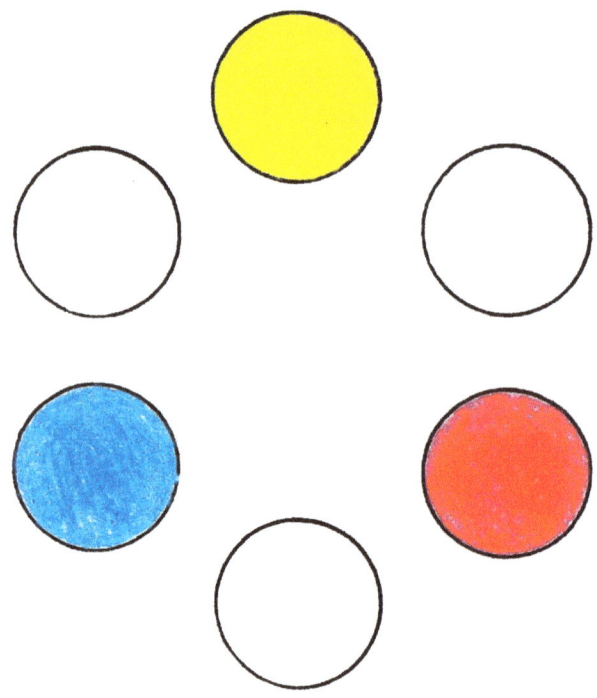

...Because
with these three colors, Blue, Red, and Yellow, you can make
every other color.
Imagine That!
You can mix two colors together and make another color.
Let's learn how to do that.

We'll start with your Blue crayon and Yellow crayon
So put them beside you and let's begin
our journey into learning the secrets of
Color Magic.

We are going to color three circles..... Circle #1
first.   Color Circle #3 next, (that's out of counting
order but color it next anyhow).
Then on the next page we will color Circle #2.

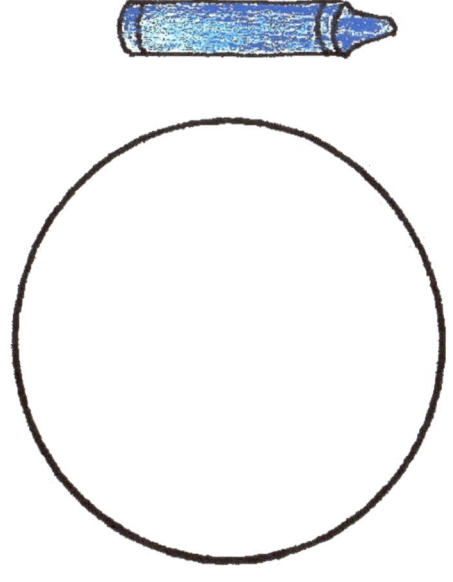

First, color Circle #1,
above
with your Blue crayon.

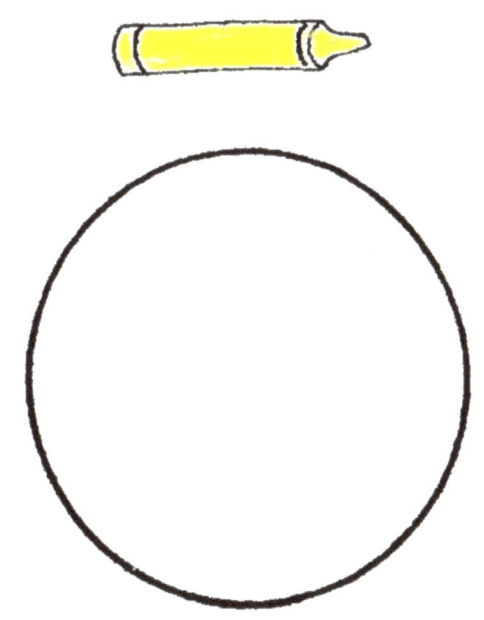

Now, color circle #3
above
with your Yellow crayon.

Now....get ready, we're going to color Circle #2 so
go to the next page and learn how the Secret
Trick of 'Primary Colors begins.......

In Circle #2, first use your Yellow Crayon again.

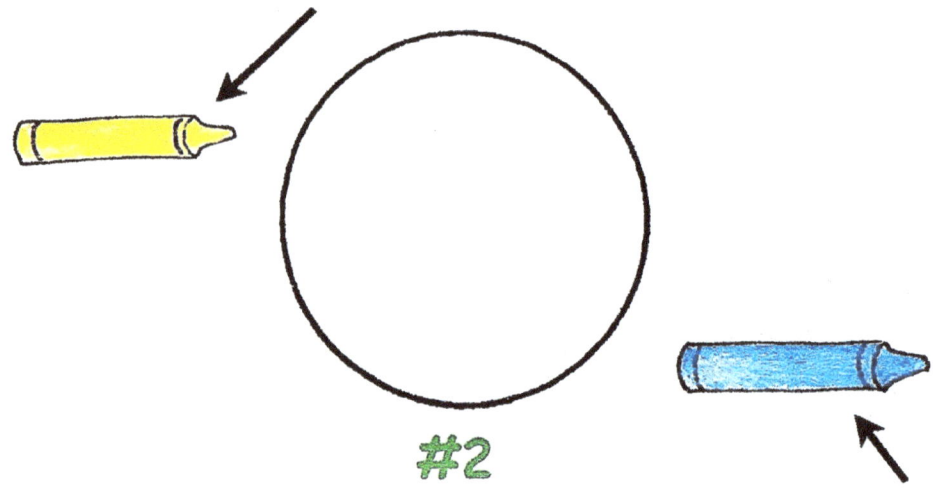

#2

Then, to make this 'Color Magic Trick' happen, use your BLUE crayon to color ON TOP of the YELLOW color in Circle #2.
You may have to layer colors more than once to get the full color.

There you are, Mates! You've learned the first Magic Trick of Primary Colors. You have made the

color...Green!

And now you know the Artist's Secret of mixing colors to make another color.

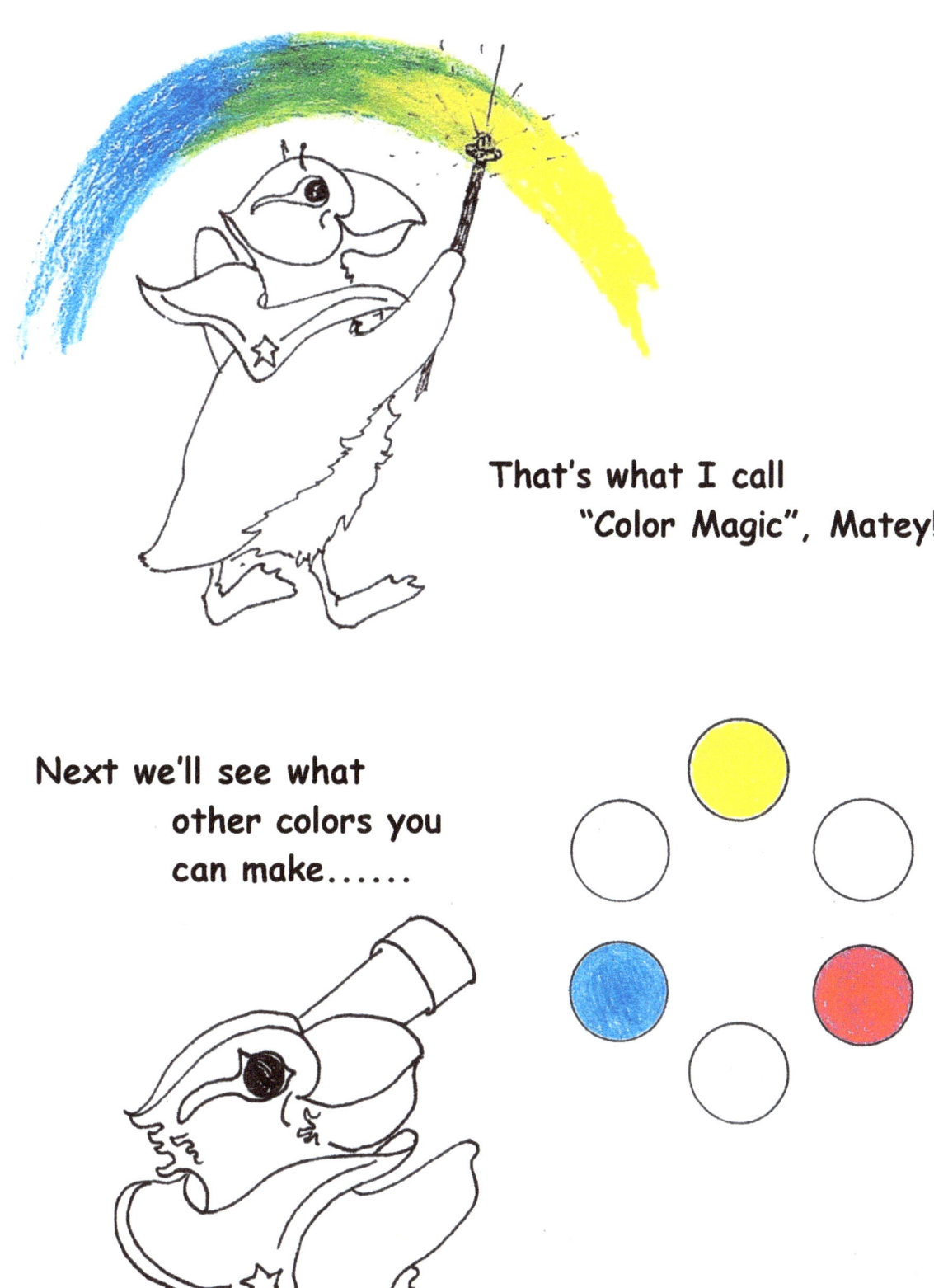

That's what I call
     "Color Magic", Matey!.

Next we'll see what
        other colors you
        can make......

Color this circle with your 'Primary' Yellow Crayon.

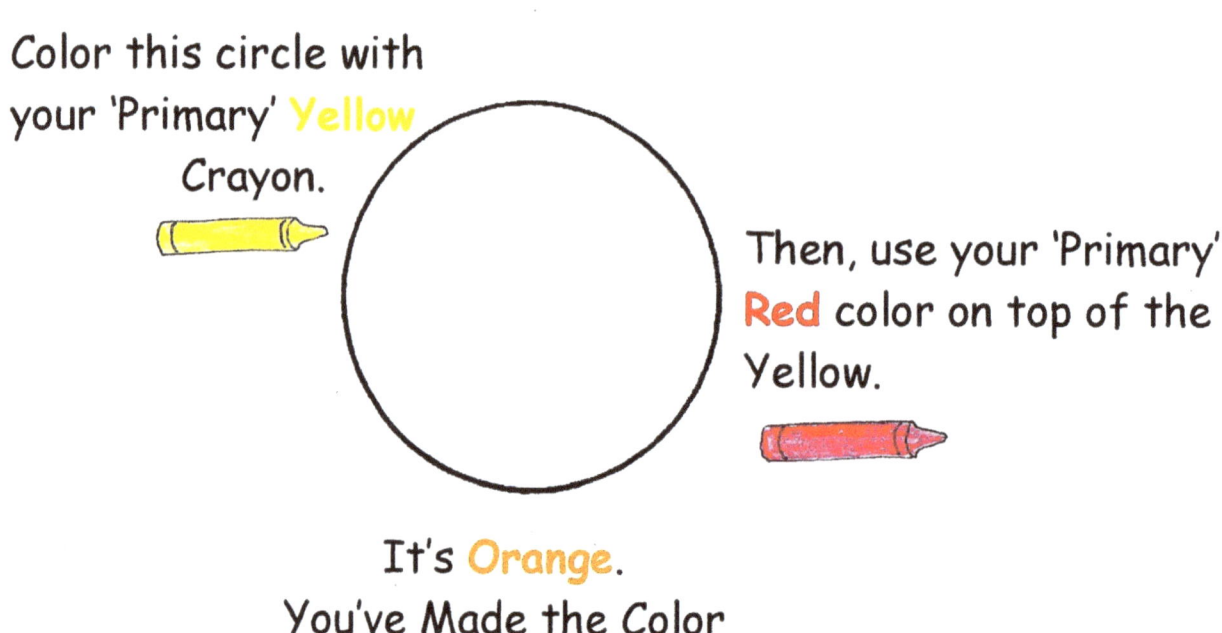

Then, use your 'Primary' Red color on top of the Yellow.

It's Orange.
You've Made the Color
Orange!.

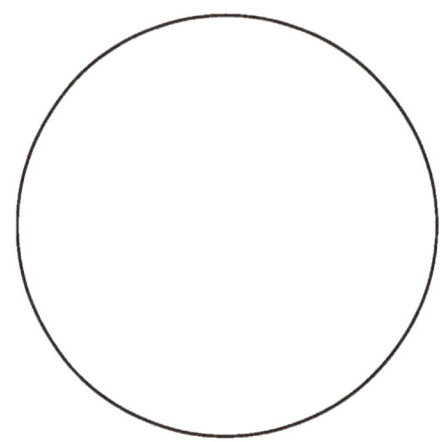

Try practicing again here. Remember, it's OK to layer yellow and red several times.

Now, let's try making one more Magic Color......

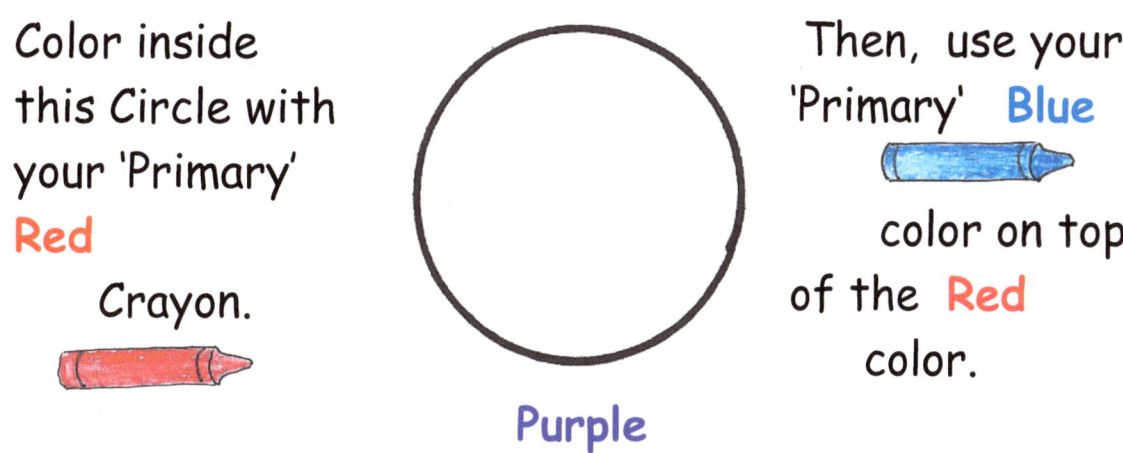

Color inside this Circle with your 'Primary' Red Crayon.

Purple

Then, use your 'Primary' Blue color on top of the Red color.

These new colors you've created are called 'secondary' colors. That's because you've added one primary color to one other primary color and have made what artists call a 'secondary' color.

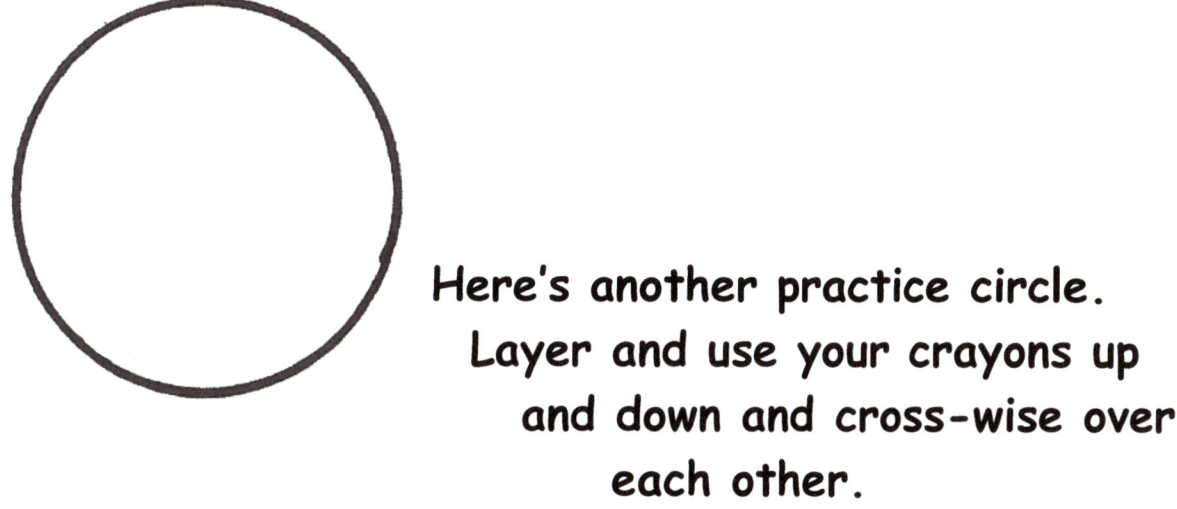

Here's another practice circle. Layer and use your crayons up and down and cross-wise over each other.

Through the magic of mixing colors, you have made 3 new colors - Green, Orange and Purple.

Now, let's put them all together......

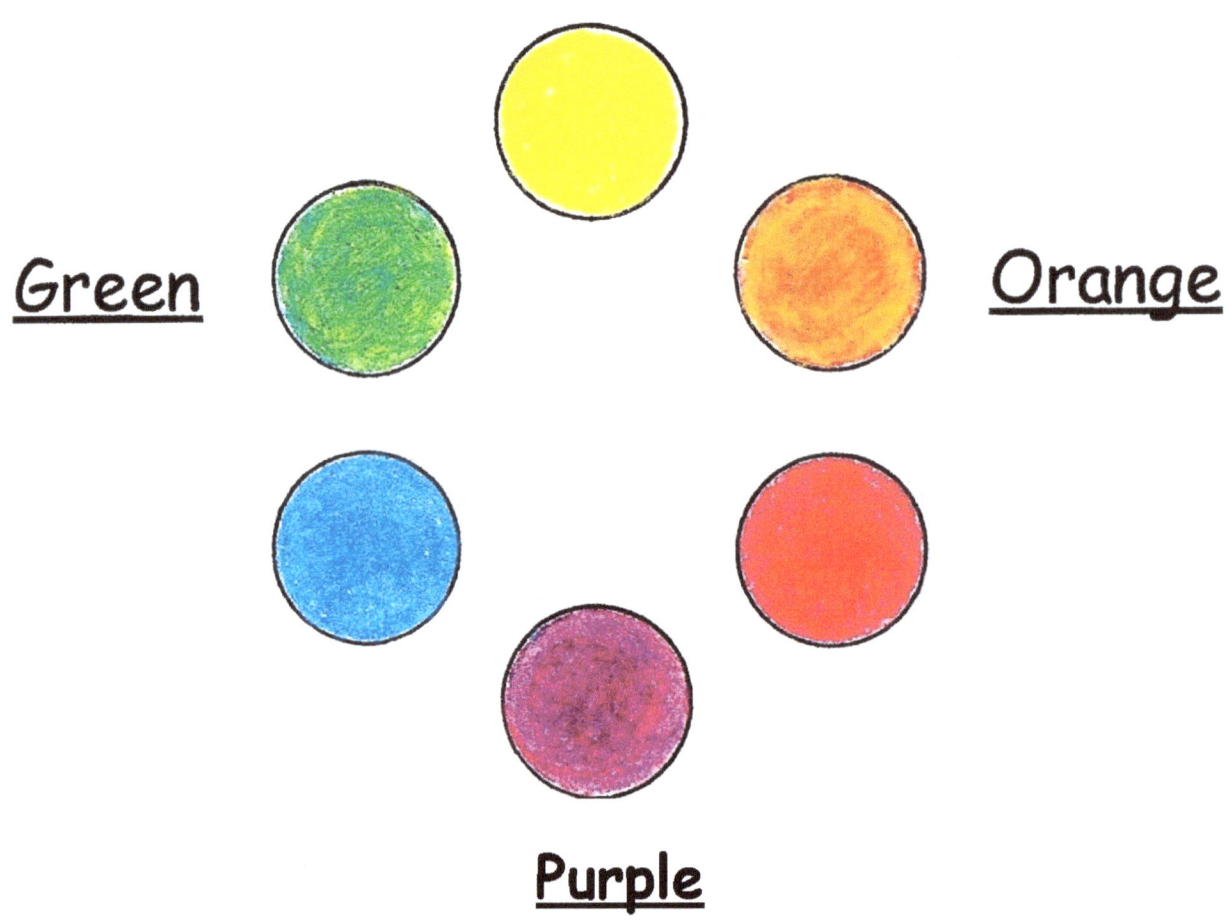

Green

Orange

Purple

You now have **6** colors. With **3** 'primary colors' you made **3** 'secondary colors'. You have made a 'Color Wheel'.
And with the magic of a 'Color Wheel', you can make many, many colors.

Have fun, mates.
Don't forget, with Art, it's
Your Show!

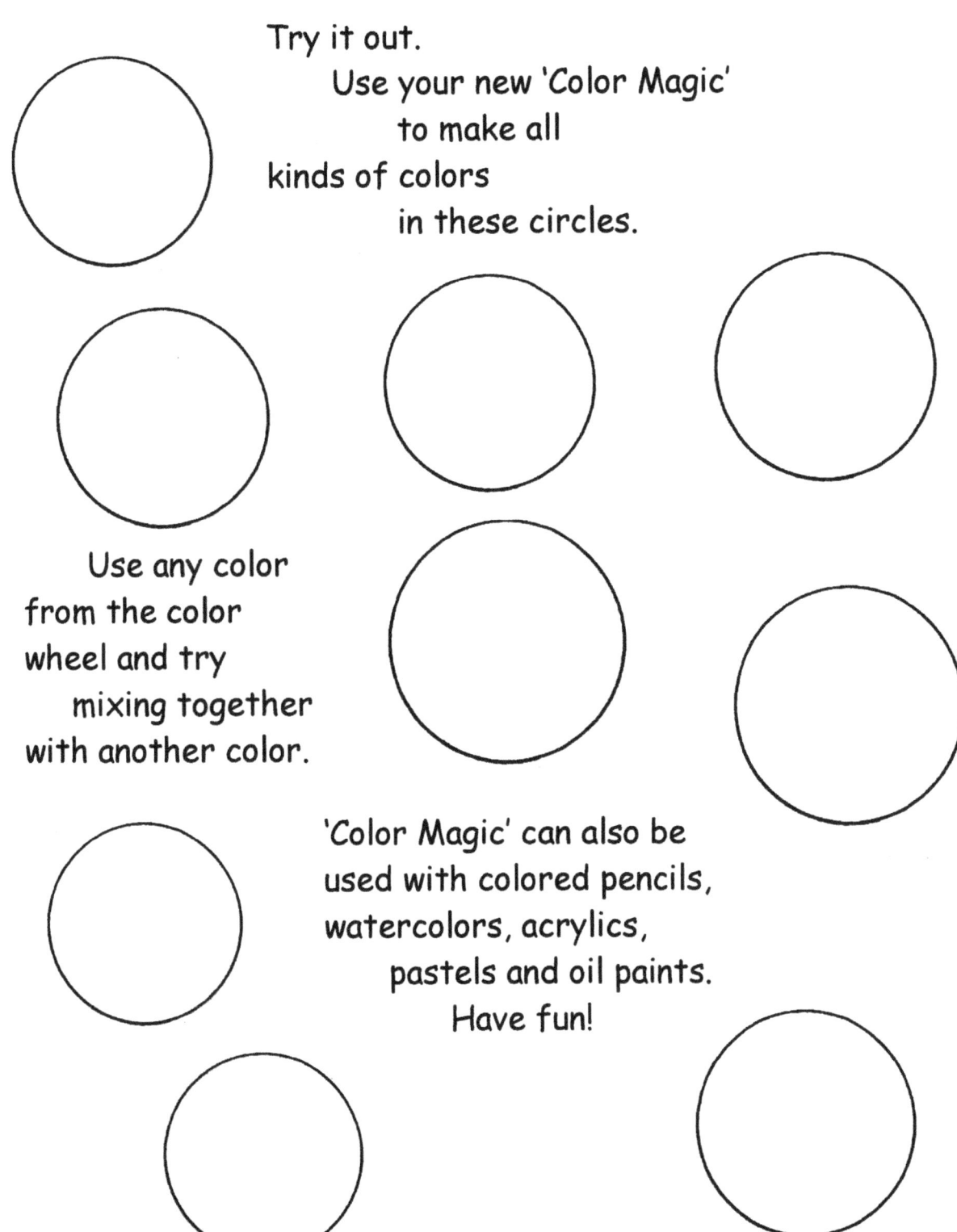

Try it out.
    Use your new 'Color Magic'
      to make all
kinds of colors
    in these circles.

Use any color
from the color
wheel and try
   mixing together
with another color.

'Color Magic' can also be
used with colored pencils,
watercolors, acrylics,
   pastels and oil paints.
   Have fun!

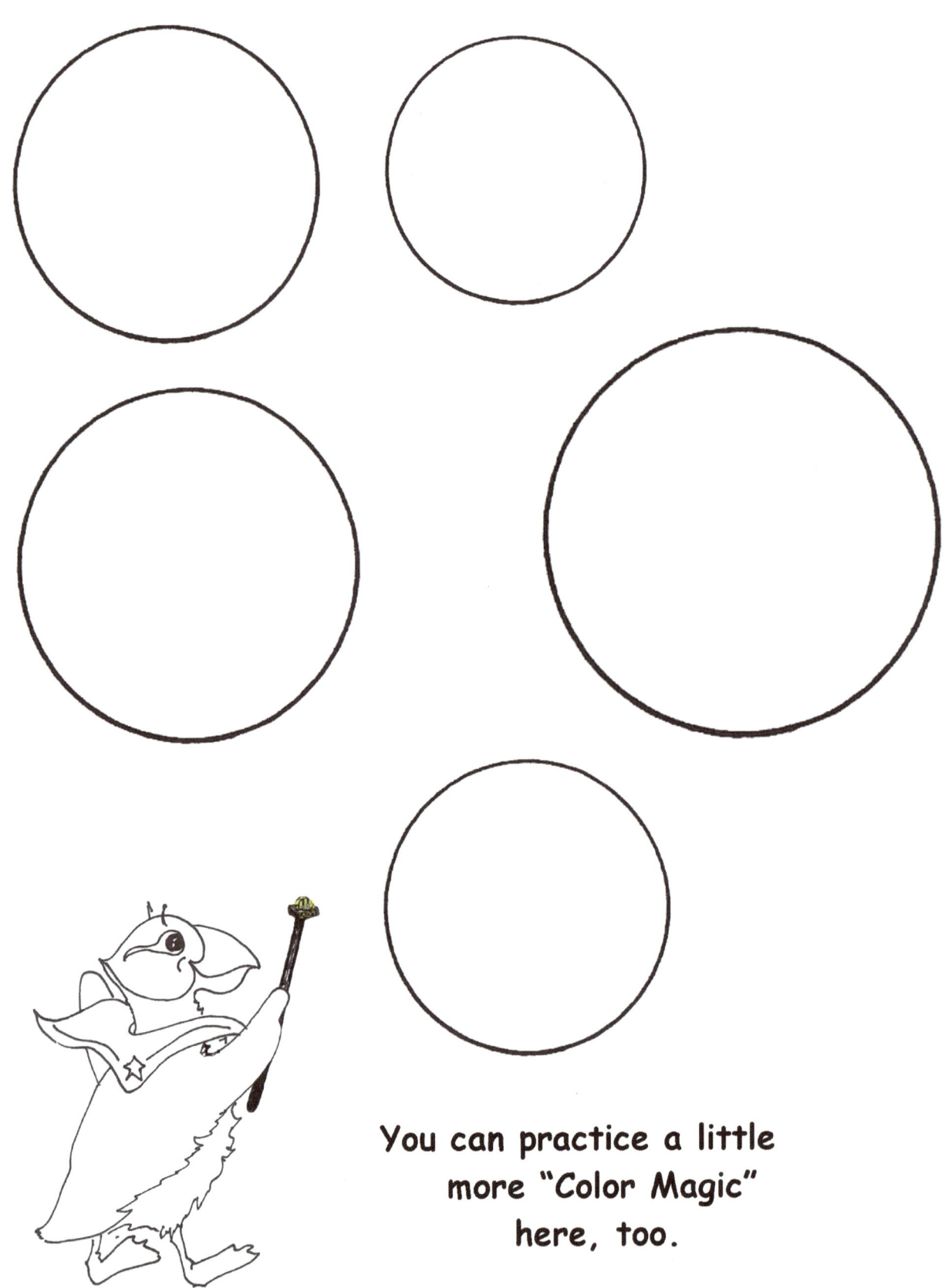

You can practice a little
more "Color Magic"
here, too.

Well, Mates, you've learned a bag full of coloring
tricks and some 'Color Magic' using crayons. Now you
can have fun coloring books and making your
own colors.

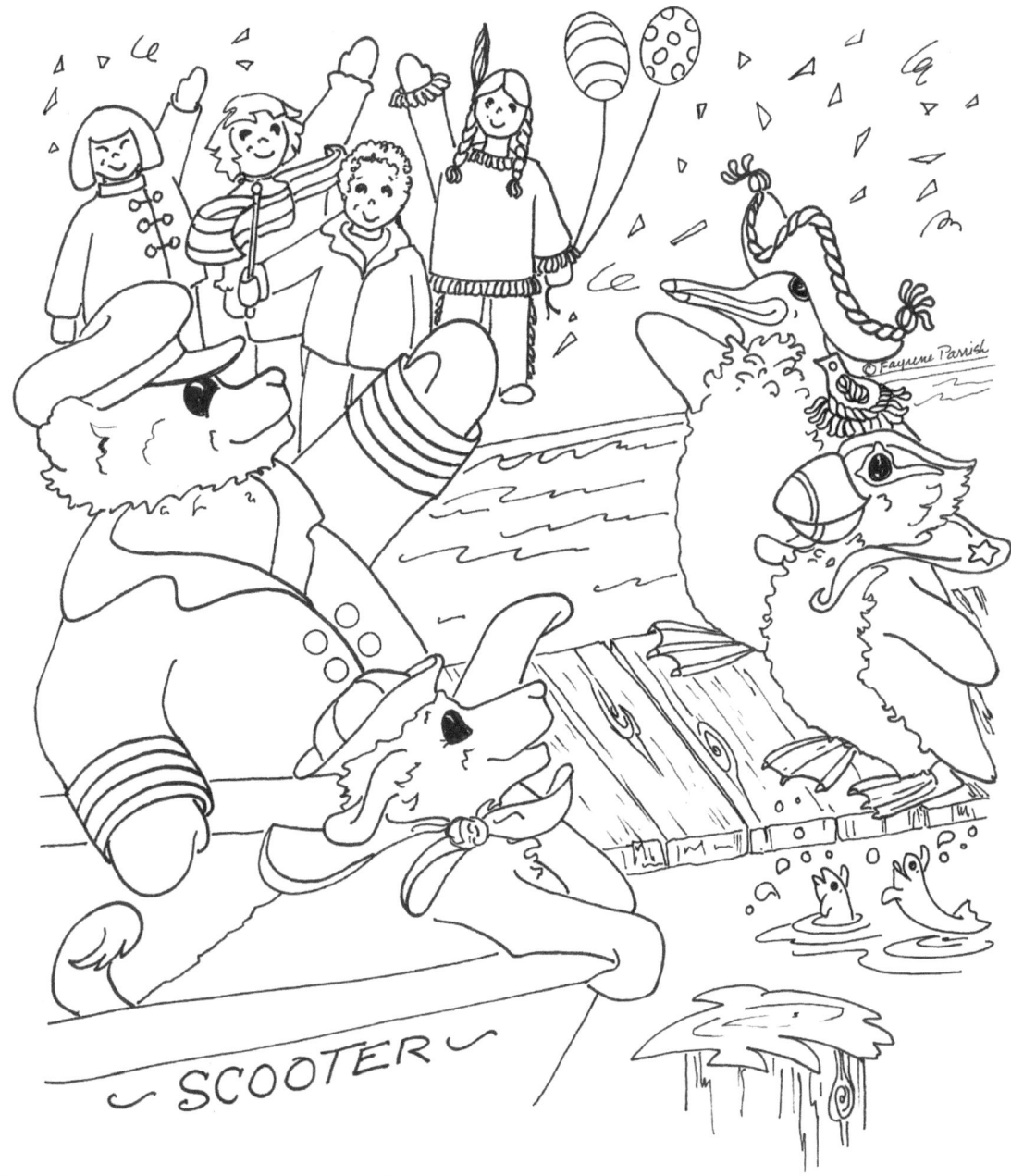

See you on our next **'Learning Adventure.'**
Until then, safe sailing.....may the sea be
smooth and the wind at your backs.
'The Shipmates'

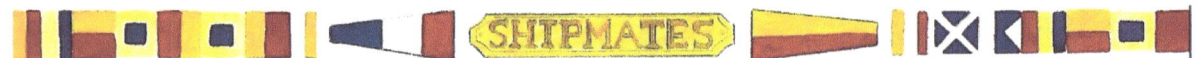

"Boat Talk" – A Nautical Glossary

Aboard – describes a place in or on a boat

Admiral – A very important, high ranking Naval Officer

Ahoy – same as saying "Hello"

Anchor – (when used as a noun)* a heavy metal <u>hook</u> that digs into the bottom of the sea to hold the boat in place

Anchor – (when used as a verb)* to secure, or 'anchor' a boat to the ocean bottom using the heavy metal hook

Ashore – on shore; on the beach, as in "I'm going ashore today."

Bow – the front of the ship

Captain – officer in command of the boat or ship

Chart – a map used on a boat to find the direction in which to travel

Crew – those living on, working and running a boat or ship

First Mate – aboard 'Scooter', it's the Captain's helper

Line – a rope that is used aboard a boat

Life Vest – a safety vest to keep you afloat in the water

Mate – a friend, a buddy, a companion on board a boat or ship

Navigator – in charge of charting and setting the course or path of the boat for a safe journey

One Fathom – is six feet deep

Port – left side of boat, opposite the <u>right</u> side of boat; **and** a harbor where ships and boats enter and anchor

Porthole – a round window on a boat

Sail – (noun)* fabric designed to catch the wind and move a sailboat

Sail – (verb)** to travel on a ship, as "We are sailing"

Shanty Song – song sung by crew aboard ship while working

Shipmates – a group sharing the same ship or boat

Skipper – Captain of the boat or ship

Stern – the back of the ship

Starboard – right side of ship; opposite left side or 'port' of ship

Tacking – moving through the wind by changing direction

A **'verb' describes action and a *'noun' describes a name.

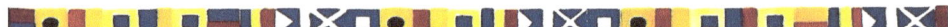

More 'Boat Talk' vocabulary will be added as we progress through 'The Shipmates Learning Adventures'.

You could maybe begin now by saying 'Ahoy, Mate' when you see a friend.

"Welcome Aboard' is the **First** in the series of "SHIPMATES LEARNING ADVENTURES. Next is 'Pancho Saves The Day', then "The Shipmates Visit the Space Needle n Seattle"....followed by Environments including:

'Sandy Shores', 'Estuaries', the 'Open Sea' and 'Rocky Shores'.
'The Shipmates Visit The Space Needle in Seattle',
All in Coloring Book format to develop 'Decision Making
Skills', 'Confidence in Decisions, 'Eye-Hand Co-ordination', and 'Graphic Reading'.

Future 'books exploring various habitats and ecosystems with 'The Shipmates'©
will take readers on many a Learning Adventure. Using Art, readers will explore Earth's many
environments and habitats as well as meet
the wondrous creatures who call those places home.

Type to enter text

Here's just a few new characters you'll soon be meeting:

'Oxy' The
Brown Pelican
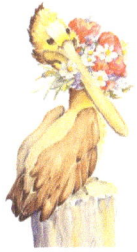
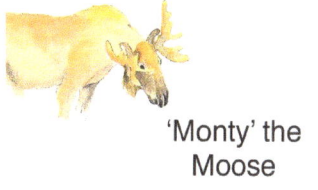
'Monty' the
Moose
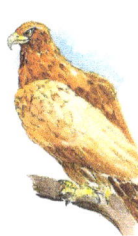
'Swifty' The
Golden Eagle

.....And a few of the Environments you'll explore and learn about:

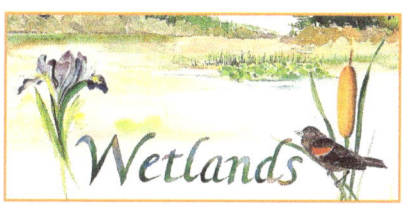
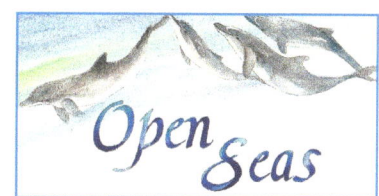
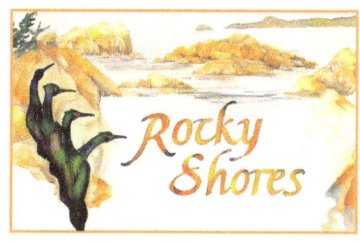
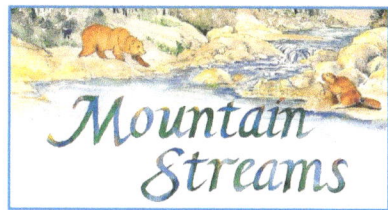
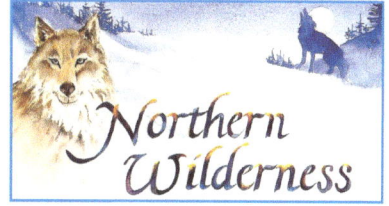

22